Let's look at
MOUTHS

First published in 2003 by Zero To Ten Limited
327 High Street, Slough, Berkshire, SL1 1TX
and 814 North Franklin Street, Chicago, Illinois 60610
This edition published under license from Zero To Ten Limited. All rights reserved.

Publisher: Anna McQuinn, Art director: Tim Foster, Publishing assistant:
Vikram Parashar

Published in the United States by Smart Apple Media
1980 Lookout Drive, North Mankato, Minnesota 56003

Library of Congress Cataloging-in-Publication Data

Sideri, Simona.
Mouths / written by Simona Sideri ; illustrated by Sheilagh Noble.
p. cm. — (Let's look at)
Summary: An introduction to the variety of
mouths found in the animal kingdom,
describing how they are used.
ISBN 1-58340-494-5
1. Mouth—Juvenile literature.
[1. Mouth. 2. Anatomy.] I. Noble,
Sheilagh, ill. II. Title. III. Let's look
at (North Mankato, Minn.)

QL857.S53 2004
591.4'4—dc22   2003058965

9 8 7 6 5 4 3 2 1

Let's look at
MOUTHS

Written by
Simona Sideri

Illustrated by
Sheilagh Noble

This is my mouth.

Open wide and look inside.

Squirrels have big teeth and strong jaws.

They are great for cracking open and eating nuts.

These gazelles have delicate lips—perfect for plucking acacia leaves without hurting themselves on the spiky thorns.

Butterflies have special mouths.

They let butterflies
suck up food.

Chameleons' tongues
are long and sticky.
They flick out quickly.

If you blink, you'll miss it!

Wild boars are hairy pigs. They have hard snouts for digging up roots.

The pelican drags its beak like a bucket to scoop up fish!

My mouth is marvellous—
for talking and laughing,
munching and licking,
smiling and making faces!